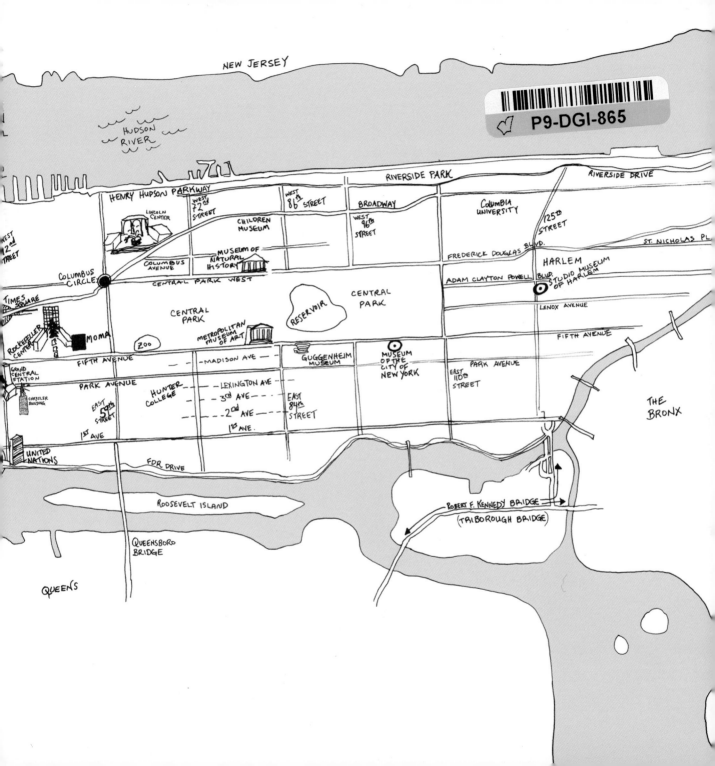

NEW JERSEY

HUDSON RIVER

P9-DGI-865

RIVERSIDE PARK   RIVERSIDE DRIVE

HENRY HUDSON PARKWAY

WEST 72nd STREET

WEST 86th STREET

BROADWAY

Columbia University

125th STREET

ST. NICHOLAS PL.

LINCOLN CENTER

CHILDREN MUSEUM

WEST 96th STREET

FREDERICK DOUGLAS BLVD.

HARLEM

WEST 72nd STREET

COLUMBUS AVENUE

MUSEUM OF NATURAL HISTORY

ADAM CLAYTON POWELL BLVD.

STUDIO MUSEUM OF HARLEM

Columbus Circle

CENTRAL PARK WEST

RESERVOIR

CENTRAL PARK

LENOX AVENUE

TIMES SQUARE

CENTRAL PARK

FIFTH AVENUE

ROCKEFELLER CENTER

MOMA

ZOO

METROPOLITAN MUSEUM OF ART

GUGGENHEIM MUSEUM

MUSEUM OF THE CITY OF NEW YORK

FIFTH AVENUE   MADISON AVE

GRAND CENTRAL STATION

PARK AVENUE

HUNTER COLLEGE

LEXINGTON AVE

EAST PARK AVENUE

EAST 110th STREET

CHRYSLER BUILDING

EAST 59th STREET

3rd AVE

2nd AVE

EAST 84th STREET

THE BRONX

1st AVE

1st AVE.

UNITED NATIONS

FDR DRIVE

ROOSEVELT ISLAND

ROBERT F. KENNEDY BRIDGE

(TRIBOROUGH BRIDGE)

QUEENSBORO BRIDGE

QUEENS

ABC in NYC

ALL 'BOUT CITIES

Murray Hill Books LLC
www.murrayhillbooks.com

Aa

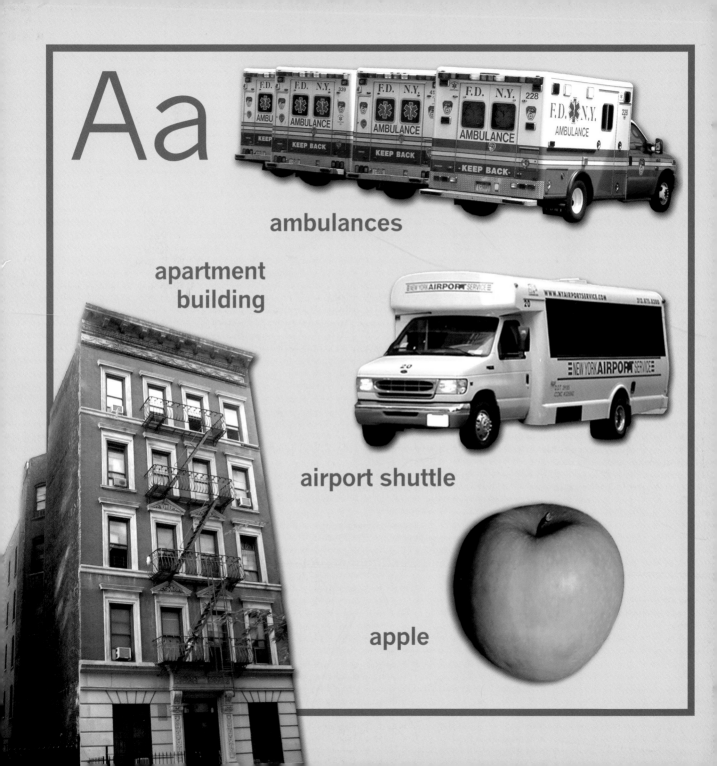

ambulances

apartment
building

airport shuttle

apple

Bb

bagel

bench

Brooklyn Bridge

bus stop

buses

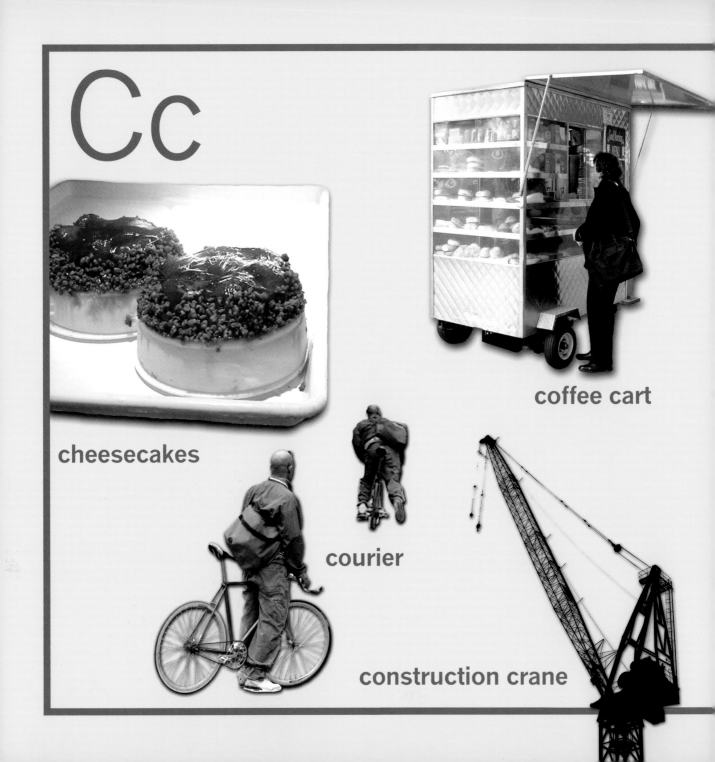

Cc

cheesecakes

coffee cart

courier

construction crane

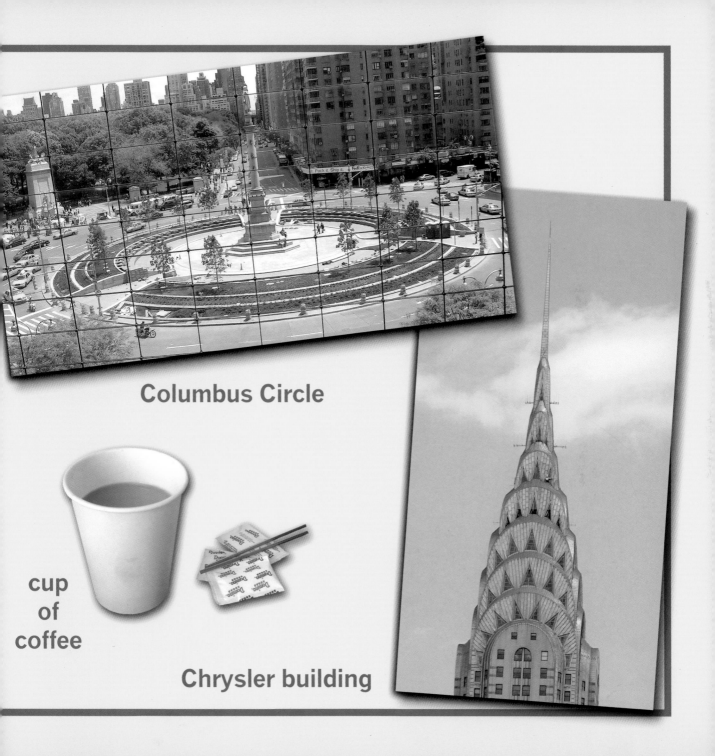

Columbus Circle

cup
of
coffee

Chrysler building

Dd

double-decker bus

doorman

dumpsters

deliveryman

dog walker

Ee

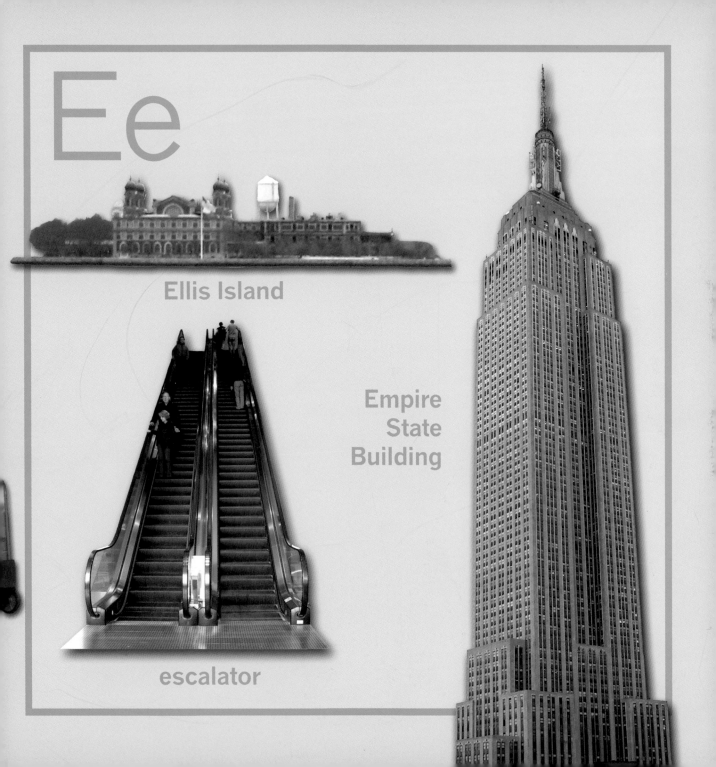

Ellis Island

escalator

Empire
State
Building

Ff

fire hydrants

fire engine

ferry

firefighters

flowers

flag

fountain

Gg

garbage truck

George Washington Bridge

graffiti

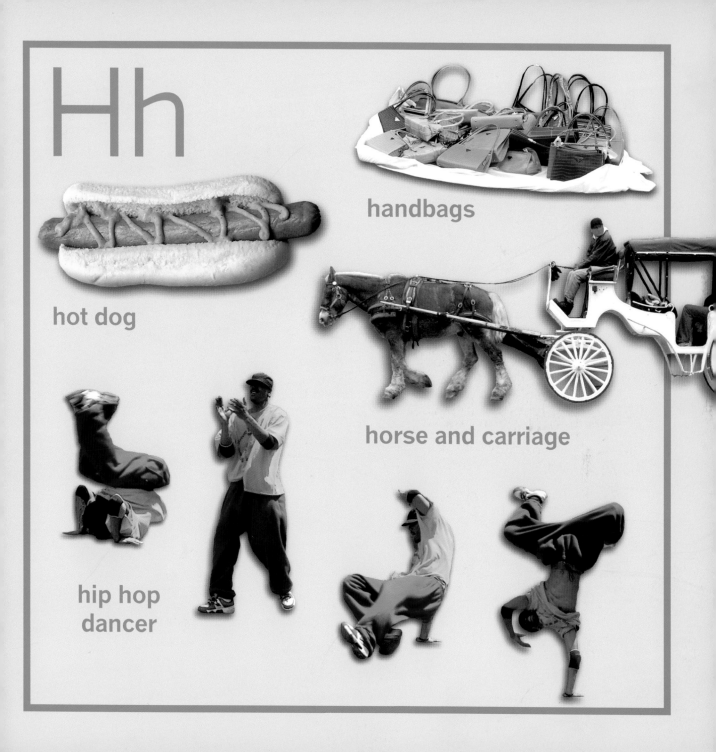

Hh

hot dog

handbags

horse and carriage

hip hop
dancer

Ii

ice cream truck

ice cream cone

ice skaters

Jj

joggers

jazz band

Kk

knish

kiosk

lamppost

license
plate

LI

Lincoln Center

library lion

Lady Liberty

Mm

money

mail carrier

musicians

menu

Metrocard®

map

manhole cover

Mets fan

Nn

newspaper vending machines

nut seller

newsstand

newspaper vendor

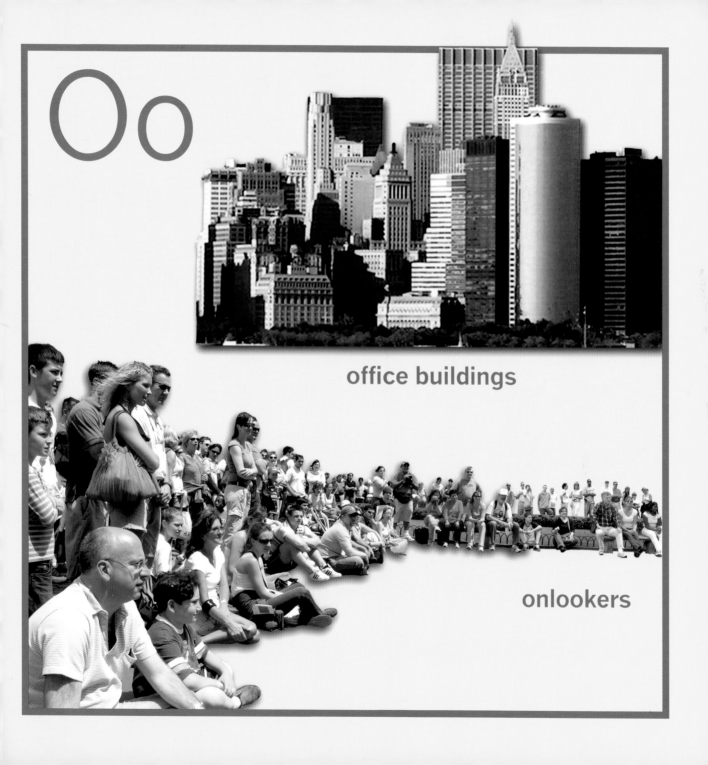

Oo

office buildings

onlookers

Pp

patrol car

pamphlet distributor

pizza pie

police officer

pretzel

plastic
pylons

planetarium

payphone

police
barriers

pigeon

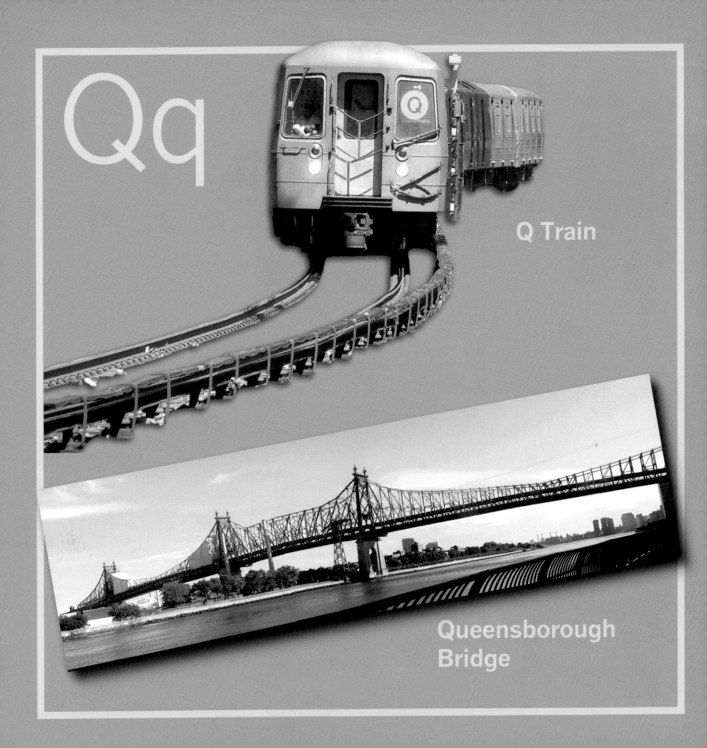

Qq

Q Train

Queensborough
Bridge

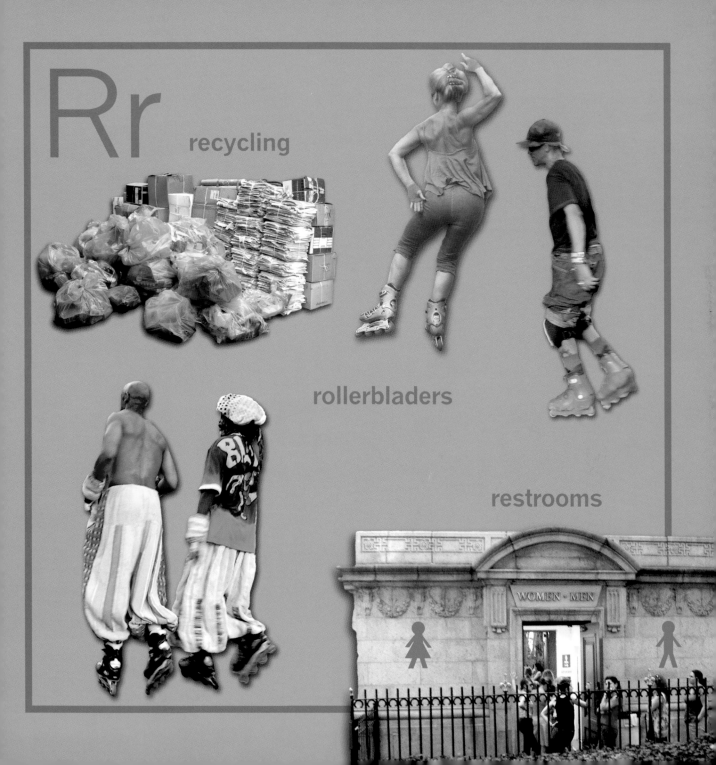

Rr

recycling

rollerbladers

restrooms

WOMEN · MEN

Ss

subway
station
stairway

ONE WAY

W 42 ST   5 AV

NO
TURNS
EXCEPT
BUSES

street
signs

scaffolding

squirrel

slice of Sicilian

stop signs

steam vent

Tt

traffic
cop

tour bus

tourists

Times Square

Keep New York City Clean

Keep New York City Clean
Don't Litter
Put It Here

trash cans

Uu

United Nations

umbrellas

Vv

vendor

Ww

window
washer

water
fountain

water
towers

walk signal

Xx

Xavier
High
School

Yy

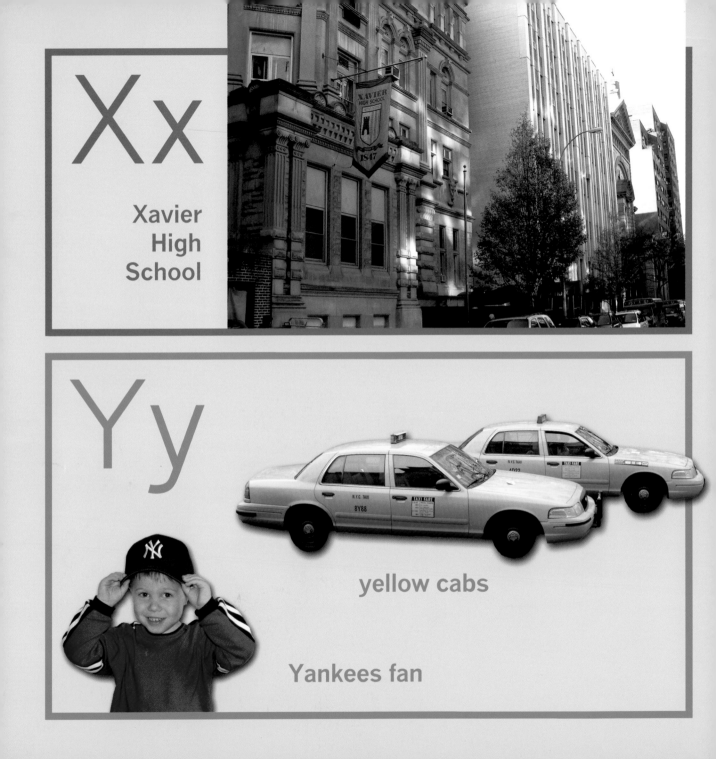

yellow cabs

Yankees fan

Zz

Zoo
animals
at
Central
Park

Zuccotti
Park

Murray Hill Books, LLC
P.O. Box 4393
New York, NY 10163

www.murrayhillbooks.com
info@murrayhillbooks.com
SAN 256-3622

Library of Congress Control Number: 2009913506
ISBN: 978-1-935139-07-2

Second Edition

Photography, Design, and Editing by Robin Segal.
"All 'Bout Cities" is a Registered Trademark.
Look for more "All 'Bout Cities" titles at:
www.allboutcities.com

www.abcinnyc.com

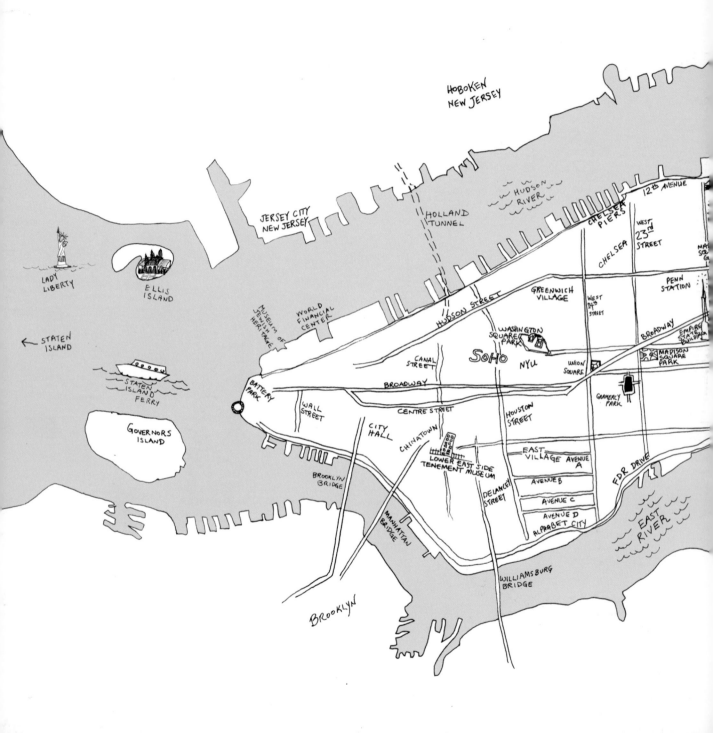